God is
Light

God is Light

Juanita Fotheringham

For since the creation of the world God's invisible qualities – His eternal power and divine nature – have been clearly seen. Romans 1:20

XULON PRESS

Xulon Press
2301 Lucien Way #415
Maitland, FL 32751
407.339.4217
www.xulonpress.com

Unless otherwise indicated, Scripture quotations taken from the Holy Bible, New International Version (NIV). Copyright © 1973, 1978, 1984, 2011 by Biblica, Inc.™. Used by permission. All rights reserved.

Printed in the United States of America.

ISBN-13: 978-1-6312-9804-2
Ebook: 978-1-6312-9805-9

Dedication

Thank you to my husband, Terry for always believing in me.

And for my Mom who lived a life, fully committed to God, no matter what.

Table of Contents

1–LIGHT 101

My father loved physics. He read physics books and would fill notepad after notepad with physics calculations—FOR FUN. One afternoon, while my brothers and I were visiting him, my father felt compelled to share his knowledge of light with us. He had pinned a stack of extra-large graph papers to his living room wall, from which he proceeded to share his presentation. On the first 18"x24" graph paper, he had a sketch of a pipe with the title, "Physics at Work in a Smoking Pipe." He apparently had an epiphany about the light that came from the lit tobacco. As he flipped through the pages of notes and calculations pinned to the wall, I found the calculations indecipherable, but the notes were fascinating. While my brothers were mumbling "When is this going to be over?" I was in awe. As he explained the properties of light, I was struck not only by the fact that every attribute he shared about light also described God, but most significantly by the fact that everything that scientists know about the universe comes from their knowledge of light.

> *This is the message we have heard from*
> *him and proclaim to you, that* God is
> light, *and in him is no darkness at all.*
> *1 John 1:5*

In studying light, I have found in this declaration from John, a profound beginning of knowledge. I will never fully understand God but I have gained confidence in His nature and in His love for us, because of the powerful message that God is light.

2—GOD IS BALANCE

I magine you are outside on an open grass area, for instance, a football field. It's a pleasant spring day, neither too hot nor too cold. The skies are clear and bright. You are standing at a goal post, what we will call the "starting point." At the opposing goal post, is a table with a bell on top. For fun, I will blindfold you, my well-sighted friend, and face you in the direction of the bell. Yes, I'll hold your sunglasses for you. Are you ready? Okay, good. Now I want you to walk to that table and ring the bell. I'm not going to coach you or nudge you, or encourage, or help you in any way. You may take your time and use your other senses, like feeling the warmth of the sun or hearing the rustle of trees to guide you. Ready? Go!

Why am I laughing? Ignore me. This is seriously funny. I should be filming this spectacle. Your arms are out like wings, and your body is wavering as if you were walking a tight rope.

Oh, and by the way, you can take the blindfold off because you are so off course that there is no way you will get to the table. I'll stop laughing in a minute.

What happened? I don't know. I do not think anyone knows. But, without sight, we automatically walk in a circle. If you are lost in the woods at night, you should stay put because without light, you will walk in circles getting nowhere. Chew a little on that realization. Darkness messes with your balance and upsets your sense of direction, which makes it difficult for you to reach your goals. Finding your way requires balance and balance requires light.

> So Jesus said to them, "For a little while longer the Light is among you. Walk while you have the Light, so that darkness will not overtake you; he who walks in the darkness does not know where he goes." John 12:35

As proved by this experiment, and the experiments of others, we know for a fact that we physically need light to walk a straight line. As previously stated, and now I further emphasize, without light we will lose our balance. In John 12:35, Jesus was letting us know that He, the Light, was the source of balance. As we walk through the other properties of light, we will see that light is so much more; but first I want to focus on balance.

Life is all about balance. We balance our checkbook to make sure we don't overspend or to confirm there are no fraudulent actions against our account. We eat balanced meals to maintain our health. We balance the tires on our cars, so they wear evenly. We need balance between work and play; too much play can cause a lack of funds to live on, or you may choose to use what funds you have for fun, rather than your home that is snowballing into disrepair. And, too much work can cause too much stress on our bodies and other areas of our life. These ordinary examples show how we need balance to provide for our basic needs. I have told my children numerous times that if Adam and Eve had not sinned, they still would have needed to tend the garden. So, we must choose to do what we need to do probably more often than doing what we want to do. We can also be out of balance in our relationships with family, friends, and faith. Balance requires knowledge of what tips the scales one way or the other. I see three ways we can lose our balance. (1) by our choices, (2) because of the choices of others, and (3) by the natural ups and downs of life; those things that just happen.

Our Choices. We make numerous choices all day long, every day. What time will I get up? Will I go to work? Will I yell at the guy who cut me off? Will I start the project due tomorrow or the exciting new project that is due in a week? Will I cook dinner or get take-out? Will I add to my credit card bill? Do I have enough in my account to buy those out-of-my-price-range shoes or do I throw caution to the wind and buy them anyway? Will I indulge myself by eating ice cream for dinner or go for a healthier option like chicken, green beans, and rice? Will I maintain my car or maintain my fun? Will I work too much or play too much? These daily choices are small but added together, they make a significant differ-ence. One year I decided to put all my spending into a spreadsheet. Two to Three times a month I chose to buy take-out for the family. At the end of the year I was shocked to find that it added up to more than $1,000. What I thought was a small choice added up to a big expense. Each time we are choosing to either put the blindfold on ourselves or to take the blindfold off. We cannot reach our goals when we choose to put the blindfold on ourselves repeatedly. At some point you will be faced with the blindfold of I-don't-have-that. The lack of anything may open us to crave that thing, which, depending on your character, may inflame your greed and have you stealing, lying, or cheating. Not good. We salivate over pleasures like ice cream, which only brings temporary pleasure. What's that saying, "A moment on your lips, forever on your hips." Ice cream is not bad until it is too much ice cream. I am fairly sure we all have our little escapes,–whether it's food or drinks or television or books or sports or video games, or any other extra-curricular activity. The fun activities are not necessarily bad. We need to have some fun. Some. Every choice we make will either hurt our balance or help maintain or increase our balance. My choice.

Ultimately, I believe to maintain balance, we need to get to the place where we can honestly live the apostle Paul's words, "I have learned to be content whatever the circumstances." He is not saying "Don't make mistakes" and "Don't be ambitious." Because we are human, we will make mistakes. And, because we need to take care of ourselves, our families, and our world, we must strive to reach our goals. We will sometimes make bad choices, but we do not need to be discouraged. Paul is encouraging us not to covet what others have. For instance, don't steal a car, you are to earn money for a car. You may not be able to earn enough for a Jaguar, but you don't *need* a Jaguar. You need transportation. Be content with the transportation within your means.

When we get ourselves off balance, look to the One who is balance. The God inspired scriptures are a light showing us, explaining to us, what balance is. One of my favorite quotes from Johann Wolfgang von Goethe reads as follows, "It's not doing the things we like to do, but liking the things we have to do, that makes life blessed." Remember we can always get the wisdom we need from God, through prayer and His word, and godly counsel. We can find our way, *in the light*, back towards balance.

The Choices of Others. Our balance can be in jeopardy from the actions of others. In these scenarios, someone is trying and often succeeding at putting the blindfold on us. For instance, someone uses your ATM card fraudulently or goes so far as to completely steal your identity.

Or you could be hit by a drunk driver or be car-jacked. Your spouse could leave you for someone else. There are so many evil things that people can do to you because evil exists. David, the shepherd who eventually became king, speaks from his own experiences of being hunted and challenged by others. How did David deal with his adversity?

David looked to his friend, the ultimate shepherd. David knew that with God, he could walk through the valley of the shadow of death, and with his eyes set on the light of God he kept his balance, stayed the course and was a conqueror. As Psalms 23 so beautifully reminds us, God will not leave us there; he shepherds us into the path of light and balance. It does not mean you won't go through the five stages of grief after a loss. It means that, amid your struggles, there is hope. God will see us through and will give us the opportunity to restore our balance. I say, "give us the oppor-tunity," because we still need to choose to follow. I believe the biggest reason people get stuck in depression is because they do not want to let go of that thing that is dragging them down. If they are dragged down by the choices of other people, through no fault of their own, it can be extremely hard to let go. Though we need to learn caution and gain wisdom from our pain, we need to leave behind the anger. Anger drags us down. To fully get away from the pain, it is important we take the step to forgive. <u>Do not</u> forget what you have learned, do not put yourself back into a bad situation, please, do not forget to stay away from the bad, but embrace the freedom that is in forgiveness. Forgiveness is powerful. It may not change the offender, but it will change you. I encourage you to forgive, let go and be free. Trust light, trust God. He is our shepherd. His rod will ward off the destroyer and his staff will gently return us to his radiance. Our shepherd will rescue us. Let Him. God has the power to help us be *overcomers*. Take it to heart, for you can have joy *despite* your pain. Joy? Yes! Joy.

The natural ups and downs of life. Our balance can also be teetering because of life circumstances. Imagine that the blindfolded man was to face a greater challenge, if the terrain were to become slippery because of rain or ice or a tree suddenly falls on his path. Conditions for which no person, in particular, is responsible for. Did you, along with half the employees at work, get laid-off and lose your job? Did you lose a loved one to death? Or lose your health?

Consider it pure joy, my brothers and sisters, whenever you face trials of many kinds.

James 1:2a

Once during a Bible study, a man raised a skeptical question about this verse in James which encourages us to consider it pure joy whenever we face trials. He asked, "So, what you're saying is that if I get in a car accident and become paralyzed, I should consider that joy?" At that moment, the leader did not have a clear answer for him. I spent the rest of the class pondering that question and realized that if being healthy is what brings us joy, then why aren't all healthy people happy? And if being wealthy is what will make us genuinely happy, then why aren't all wealthy people happy? Health and wealth are not the key to true joy. Robin Williams was an extremely talented actor and comedian, who was sought after, and the life of the party. When interviewed on talk shows, he was hilarious, incredibly, and innately. When he took his own life, he left behind a one-hundred-million-dollar estate ($100,000,000.00). He had it all *except* true joy. That joy that is infused into the depths of our heart and mind, when we invite God's light to not only be in our lives, but to influence our response to every kind of choice or circumstance. That is when God moves from a resident in our lives, to the President of our lives.

God is balance. Know that despite our shortcomings, and we all have them, against all our mistakes and the mistakes of others, and we've all made some, undeterred by who we are or where we've been, God, in all his radiance, will light our path and direct us from where we are to where we will be winners. I love the song "Just as I Am," written by Charlotte Elliot in 1835. Its timeless truth reminds us that God accepts us right where we are, right now, no matter what we have done – just as we are. He embraces us, and just as light engulfs a room, God's love surrounds us and infuses us with hope.

The word "enlighten" means to give knowledge and understanding about a subject or situation. This word states the obvious need for light to give us sight or insight. The fact that God is light is the reason why He is the one that allows us to see truth and love and joy. God is the source of illumination so that we may find our way. His light will expand your understanding.

Light provides clarity and balance. Our struggles bind and blind us. Instead of focusing on the light at the end of the tunnel, we focus on our struggles and by our own choice, we become unbalanced. Instead of absorbing light, we absorb advice from other blindfolded sources that misdirect us, rather than from the source of light. Light encourages us to catch our breath and to keep learning, training, and pushing ourselves beyond our comfort zone, no matter what hazardous circumstances come our way. Because we need balance, we will seek discipline and wise godly counsel and remain committed. Our focus must be on the light, which is Christ. Focus on the Light and you will find peace, joy, and abundant life. Jesus said that if any of us lacks wisdom, we should ask God, who gives generously to all without finding fault, and it will be given to me and to you. I like how it is expressed here:

> *The eye is a lamp of the body. If your eyes are healthy, your whole body will be full of light.* Matthew 6:22

Through our eyes, the light of God may enter our bodies. When our eyes absorb all the balance of God, we can be saturated by His divine qualities; as a result, we become more God-centered and less self-centered. Instead of repeating "me, me, me, look at me," we realize that it is not all about me. Proven fact: Self-centeredness will lead to self-destruction. Selfishness functions like a blindfold, causing us to circle around ourselves and get nowhere. Once our body is full of light, everything we do, everything we are, radiates the light and love of God to those around us. We were created to have fellowship with God and man.

> *But if we walk in the light, as he is in the light, we have fellowship with one another, and the blood of Jesus, his Son, purifies us from all sin.* I John 1:7

Light, balance and fellowship with God are intertwined. Whether your balance is challenged by your choices, the choices of others or the circumstances of life; God has provided us with the keys to a balanced life. When you seek the Light of God, through pray (ask and you will receive), His scripture (seek and you will find) or godly counsel (knock and the door will be opened to you), you will find balance. And your balance will be made complete when you have fellowship with one another. .

This is where we start. As we discover each property of light, my prayer is that you will not only see that light has a purpose *in* your life and *for* your life, but that you will be inspired to see *the* true Light with a capital L. Seek balance. God is balance.

3–GOD IS CONSTANT

In the early days of my work, in large office space planning, we would dedicate a room for computers. This room would be anywhere from the size of an office to the size of a banquet hall. It depended on how much information a business needed to process. The large computer rooms would have a raised floor, made of removable panels (2' by 2'), situated above the concrete floor (about 12" to 18" high). The tiles were set into a strong grid, with posts at the corners of each panel, to support the weight of all the hefty equipment that would eventually be housed on top. This room would even have its own dedicated electrical panel. From that panel, all the electrical outlets for the computer cabinets would be sourced. In between the raised floor and the concrete floor, a multitude of computer cables would run from one cabinet to another. Imagine the mess of cables under your computer desk right now. Now multiply that number times…well, allot. Some IT guy would have to keep track of that tangled web of cables (this would be the room-wide-web of cables that pre-dated the world-wide-web).

Bear with me, there's more. Since water is not friends with electricity or computers, the required fire sprinklers on the ceiling had to be exchanged for a halon system. The substance halon is what is used in hand-held fire extinguishers. In this case, a corner of the room or a closet contained the large tanks of halon, to be piped through the sprinkler heads if there were a fire. The room also needed its own dedicated air conditioner for maintaining the temperature 24/7. Not only did the cabinets generate allot of heat, but they needed to be kept cool enough so that they would not overheat. And the computations that these rows of large, heavy, computer cabinets produced is nothing in comparison to what our laptops do today. Imagine that. I piled on all that lengthy description of what a computer room used to be verses what it is today, because I want you to sense the massive difference between then and now.

Now offices have much smaller computer or "server" rooms, sometimes as small as a closet. The computer server is used for file storage and sharing of files, while the actual computing, digitizing, and programing are housed in our central processing unit or CPU. The CPU is the small computer cabinet that fits under your desk. (To quote one of my favorite comedians, Angela Johnson, "Just one.") And, even more compact, for our personal use, computers have been compressed down into our cellphones, which can access the internet, store files, and transmit data. The gap between the first computers and our computers today, in terms of size and ability, is thousands of miles apart. Things can <u>change</u> allot.

As I sit here in front of my computer, I am often baffled at how someone's mind came up with the idea that a string of figures—just zeros and ones—could create every imaginable possibility that we now see on our monitors. My limited knowledge cannot believe that this works or how this is possible. Obviously, it does work, but it does not make any sense to me. Whether or not it makes sense, I gladly take advantage of the incredible abilities of my computer, while computer programmers continue to expand its possibilities.

You see, we keep expanding and changing and growing. Though I still have limited knowledge of light, I want to take advantage of what others know. As I said in the beginning, everything scientists know about the universe comes from their knowledge of light. I am not only baffled at the properties of light, but at one's ability to measure its speed. My father worked for North American Rockwell, an aerospace company, eventually purchased by Boeing. He worked in the Autonoetic Department. His job was to calibrate the instruments that calibrated the instruments used by the engineers. I shared earlier, that it was my father's lecture about light that spurred me to think more in-depth about the scriptures many references that "God is light". In that lecture, my father shared with us that the only constant in the universe is light, and everything else in the universe is measured against the speed of light. I'm going to repeat it because this was a defining moment for me. The only *constant* in the universe is LIGHT. People change, the earth changes, computers change, everything changes, *except* light. And, because of the constant nature of light, scientist measure everything else in the universe, against the speed of light. Put your closed hands on either side of your head and slowly spread your fingers as your mouth attempts to make the sound of an explosion. Astounding, right? It was for me. Yes, it is that moment of truth. The only constant in the universe is light; the one constant in the universe is God, because God is Light.

> *Jesus Christ is the same yesterday and today and forever.* Heb. 13:8

There is great comfort in knowing that God never changes. For me, it is like knowing that just as I can always count on my mother's love; I know that I can count on God. I may not understand the changes going on around me, but I know His love for me will never end. He will constantly pursue me, even though I should be the one pursuing him. God will faithfully be with me. He will allow me to learn from my mistakes and grow and laugh and cry. He will be there to share in my joys and pick-me-up when life knocks me down. Forever my guide, my friend, my God. I had a friend who wisely noted that one thing we can always count on in life, is change. From birth to old age, we change. Seasons change, finances change, what's in-style absolutely changes, cars and computers and things change. Change is inevitable. Thankfully, *God never changes.*

As I ponder this incredible truth, I hear the song, "Great is thy faithfulness, O God my Father." This song reminds us that no matter what, God is constantly faithful. No shadow or overcast sky can change the fact that his light still shines. God does not change. He does not fail us. He has always been and always will be. Day after day after day, His mercies get me through the difficulties of life. All that I need, His hand provides. "Great is thy faithfulness, Lord, unto me." Yes, to me. I am a micro-spec in the universe, yet I matter. You matter. Through every season of life, summer fun and winter snow, through the planting in spring and the harvest in the fall, the sun, moon, and stars in their life above, join with all nature, in their different forms and purposes, all expressing how GREAT is His faithfulness! Great is His love and mercy to me.

God pardons my sins and gives me a peace that passes understanding. God's presence in my life gives me true joy, and when life tries to suck the joy out of me, he guides me to the right path. He gives me strength for my days and *bright hope* for tomorrow. There's nothing better than that. Thousands of blessings from our constant faithful God.

Sing it with me.

> *Great is Thy faithfulness*
> *Great is Thy faithfulness*
> *Morning by morning new mercies I see*
> *All I have needed Thy hand hath provided*
> *Great is Thy faithfulness, Lord, unto me.*

Life is full of change. Weather, ecology, day-light, and temperatures change four times a year. And each year has varying degrees of mild or extreme seasons. Economies, leadership, and fads change. Flowers bloom and grow. New people and animals are born, yet everything grows old and withers and dies. Imagine if all the people who ever lived, never died – talk about overcrowding. Even the earth itself, our largest living, breathing, ever-changing basis for life, will continue to grow old and will eventually die. But God, who never changes and will never die, has a new heaven and a new earth for us. We will one day open our eyes to the light of heaven, in the heavenly city that needs no sun because the glory of God gives it light. It does not matter if things change. As we have discussed, change is inevitable. What matters is where we focus our attention. What matters most is that we can have confidence in God. Confidence in His constant nature. Pastor Kyle shared so beautiful this morning, insights from Psalm 62, that we can have confidence in God because He alone is our victory – the battle belongs to God. God alone is our refuge – we cannot find refuge in people or wealth, they are illusions. And finally, God alone is our true salvation – our freedom from the fear of change.

Seek balance and focus on our constant, ever-present, loving God who has brought light to the universe, making all things visible. You will see Light makes all the difference in the world. The Lord God Omnipotent Reigns! YES!

4—GOD IS LIFE

Most of us remember learning about photosynthesis in elementary school. I remember filling two paper cups with soil. We put marks on a popsicle stick and stuck it in the dirt against the edge of the cup to measure the growth of the little seed we had planted. One cup we placed on our kitchen windowsill and the other in a closet. Both were watered equally. The seed in the closet peeked through the soil but withered and died. The plant on the windowsill grew and became whatever it was I planted–because frankly, I don't remember what kind of seed it was. I do remember that with light, that seed continued to grow.

Upon googling "define photosynthesis" I got this: "The process by which green plants and some other organisms use sunlight to synthesize foods from carbon dioxide and water. Photosynthesis in plants generally involves the

25

green pigment chlorophyll and generates oxygen as a byproduct." In 1779, the Dutch scientist, Jan Ingenhousz published his discovery of photosynthesis. Ingenhousz found that life and growth are not possible without light. Now, consider the fact that people and plants must coexist. We need oxygen and we give off carbon dioxide. Plants need carbon dioxide and give off oxygen. Human beings and plant life are interdependent. We cannot have one without the other. What we as human beings have in common with plants is our need for sunlight and water. Light is one of the most important sustainers of life.

Sunlight provides vitamin D, which we need to be healthy. Vitamin D or sunlight builds our immune system;–that's why colds are more common in the winter. Less sunlight means less vitamin D, so our immune system weakens. Vitamin D strengthens our bones and muscles because it enables the absorption of calcium. Put on some sunscreen and make sure your children get outside to play and absorb sunlight. Sunlight serves also as an anti-inflammatory for our lungs and helps regulate our blood pressure. So, we need to romp in the sun with our children. Sunlight is also known to regulate kidney function and to be an anti-depressant. Knowing the benefits of exercise and sunlight gives new meaning to "take a hike." Yes, get out of there, stop dwelling on your worries, and take a hike. A vitamin D deficiency can cause you to feel hungry all the time and can possibly be linked to Alzheimer's disease. The less sunlight there is, the less vitamin D. As important as it is that we do not get too much sun, it is equally important to get out in the sun. But do not forget the sunscreen. We need light. I'll say it again. Light is an important sustainer of life.

Jesus said, 'I am the light of the world. Whoever follows me will never walk in darkness but will have the light of life.'
John 8:12

Jesus is the light of life. Light of life – the source of health and growth. <u>God is life</u>.

Photosynthesis was discovered in 1779. The Gospel of John was written, most likely, before the year 100. Do you see how the Scriptures are God inspired? Inspired by the Light of Life. Jesus is the light of life. God of life – the source of health. Sounds like such a simple statement. God is light.

In Chapter Two we expanded our foundation, exploring that it is the light of God that not only allows us to see, but also to navigate. He is our source of direction, the compass we need so that we may avoid walking in circles.

> *Trust in the Lord with all your heart and lean not on your own understanding. In all your ways acknowledge him, and he will direct your path.* Prov. 3:5-6.

He has the best path for *the best life*. <u>God is balance</u>.

In Chapter Three we are encouraged by the fact that God is constant. He consistently pursues us, provides guidance through prayer and scripture, and wants us to have life, life more abundantly. God will always be there for us. God gives us confidence because <u>God is constant</u>.

Now add to those truths, that God is the source for us to grow and flourish and be the strongest and most beautiful version of ourselves. Think about it. Absorb the immensity of who God is. How important it is for us to seek him, to reach for him. Be enlightened by his Word.

In him was life, and the life was the <u>light</u>
of men. The light shines in the darkness,
and the darkness has not overcome it.
John 1:4-5

The scripture says, "In him was life." God is
the source of life, and without light, nothing can
grow. Nothing is sustained. The passage goes on
to say, "And the life was the light of men." It gives
me chills to try to grasp all that it means to say
that God is light. This is big. This is sustaining.
This *is* living the best life.

Before David was a king or a psalmist, he was a
simple shepherd. His father did not even put him
in the line-up of sons when Samuel came looking
for God's choice for the King of Israel. Samuel
had to ask, "Are these all of your sons?" David, the
youngest, was out tending the family's sheep. By
human standards he was a simple, little guy of no
great importance. But, as God said, "Man looks at
the outward appearance, but the Lord looks at the
heart." (I Sam. 16:7) And here is what was in the
heart of David, the shepherd boy, an unexpected
depth in his declaration:

The Lord is God, and he has made his light to shine upon us. Ps. 118:27

From divine inspiration David has expressed that God has made his light of guidance, faithfulness, and growth, to shine … on … *us!* Do you feel yourself wilting from the pressures of your days? Step into the light. Seek *Gods restoring light.* Expel the carbon, the waste from your system: your burdens. God will transform those burdens into life-sustaining oxygen, the breath of life. Darkness does not overcome us, because it cannot overcome light. Light overcomes darkness. Light overcomes the negative and gives us life, life more abundantly.

In the beginning God created the heavens and the earth. Darkness was over the surface of the earth and God said, "Let there be light". Light had to be next because without light, there is no life. What I hope I have clearly expressed is this:

Light is life, God is light, <u>God is life</u>.

GOD IS WITHOUT MASS

I love the word "grasp." I'm sure you already know that grasp means to seize and hold firmly. Grrrrasp! The word even sounds intense and is powerful. I want to grasp life! Sounds dynamic and inspiring, right? Babies and toddlers need to grasp everything, it is how they learn what things are. Are they light or heavy? Are they hot or cold? Can I chew on them or eat them or choke on them? Can I use them, or do I throw them away? Will I love it or hate it? Will it love me back? Can I control it, or will it control me? As adults we want all our questions answered and we want to control everything. We want to seize life and hold it firmly in the grasp of our hands. But sometimes we hold too tight and crush or harm what we thought we had control of. Often things change and what we thought was in our grasp slips away. I have learned that I am not totally in control. I am

31

grateful to know that God is in control and His grasp is firm and gentle and ever-present.

When I was in my early twenties, my father moved to Florida to retire. After about fifteen years, he realized he missed being near his family and decided to move back to California. So, my sister-in-law Christine and I started to search for a home within his budget. Over several Saturdays, we drove out to prospective cities, looked at homes, and evaluated the conveniences and conditions for my father. One Saturday, Christine was not available, so I drove off with my two children. For the life of me, I cannot remember the name of the city or where we ended up. The place was located, for all intents and purposes, in "the boonies." The city had two neighborhoods, one to the south of the main street, the other to the north. The south looked clean and inviting, the north appeared less desirable. The realtor I spoke to, tried to convince me to purchase a lot on the north side. The lot was dirt cheap (pun intended) and full of possibilities. The realtor even had a mobile home that he said would not cost much to relocate to this lot. Hum, I had to think about the proposal. After we left him, I started to pray. I wanted to find a place that we would want to visit. I wasn't sure what to think of what we saw. Although incredibly quiet and peaceful, the place seemed almost too quiet and too peaceful.

As I was driving out of that neighborhood, I noticed the fire department. Surely, they could give me insight into my question, "Is this a good place for a little old man to call home?" So, I parked my van, gathered my children, and walked up to the firehouse door. I stood there for a minute or two looking at the door. Do we just walk right in? If this were a police station, I certainly would. But there were no windows and fireman usually live here, right? I awkwardly knocked on the door. As the door flung open, a nice fireman appeared, looking perplexed. I'm sure it was uncommon to have visitors, and here stood a woman with her kids knocking on their door. I explained my situation, how my father wanted to move to California but had a small budget. He needed to be within reasonable driving distance of family. I explained that we were interested in a lot, but something felt off about the neighborhood.

Thank God I knocked on the firehouse door. The captain informed me that the families to the south were nice retirees, who were often robbed by the drug addicts to the north. The north was quiet now, because they were still sleeping off their drinking and carousing of the night before. Clearly, this would not be the kind of place for a little old man to make his home nor for sweet visits by his grandchildren. The captain took me to a map on the wall, directing me to drive to the retirement town of Hemet. I thanked him repeatedly and off we drove.

As we were nearing the city, I began to pray again. Where exactly should I go? And then I saw beams of light bursting through the clouds. Like the wisemen, I headed in the direction of those beams, to where they hit the earth. You may mock me for putting so much value upon a natural occurrence on a rainy day, but the long and the short of it is, we found a home for my dad. Great story for me. I love to share it because, I was in a tough situation, but I prayed and then I followed the light. But digging deeper, I began to ponder about the beams of light. From a distance, the beams were very bold, well defined, and direct. Once I was next to and inside the beams, I could no longer distinguish them as separate from the daylight. Where did they go?

Grab a flashlight and let's experiment. Turn-off the lights, preferably when it is dark outside, so that we are in a truly dark room. Turn on your flashlight and try to grab some light. You cannot grab anything because light has no mass. You can cover the flashlight with your fingers, but that will not stop the light from shining. You may feel some warmth and you will see the glow of light shine through the pink outer flesh of your fingers. You cannot taste it or smell it or grasp it. It's just there.

The same is with sunlight, it's just there. We know it provides balance, life, and health. And though we continue to rotate away from the sun, it is still constantly there, ready to greet us at the dawn of another day. Similarly, though I cannot grasp God, I know He is constantly there, and I can absorb His healing power. I can grow and bloom into the person I am meant to be, as I seek His truths and balance. I cannot taste him or smell him, but I sense the warmth of his presence when I walk in his light. I cannot grasp God. No one can. He is just there. Always, ever-present, right where I am; right where you are. And no matter what the world may say or do or think, they cannot stop God. When I can tune out the fact that people are watching me, and I can place my "cool card" out of sight; it is during those treasured moments when I can joyfully bask in his glory. I can sing like no one is listening, I can dance like no one is watching, I can laugh and cry and lift my hands and worship. Did all the difficulties of life go away? No, but even though I walk in the valley of the shadow of death, I do not need to fear because my most powerful, greater God is there with me. He will shine his light to illuminate the way. As in the old song "In the Garden" by C. Austin Miles, he walks with me and he talks with me, and he tells me I am his own. And the joy we share, as we live this life on earth, is inexplicably amazing. God will walk with me through it all. I cannot grasp light in my hand, and I cannot grasp God, neither figuratively nor physically in my hand, but God has me in the grasp of his hand. And, when I invite and allow God's Holy Spirit to come and dwell inside of me, then I have a touch of His light. I have God's joyful *balance* to guide me, the power of His *constant* presence to empower me, and His restoring light of *life* in me, that I may bloom and grow. Victory is mine because of the one who holds me.

So that Christ may dwell in your hearts
through faith. And I pray that you,

being rooted and established in love,
may have power, together with all the
Lord's holy people, to grasp how wide
and long and high and deep is the love
of Christ, and to know this love that
surpasses knowledge—that you may be
filled to the measure of all the fullness
of God. Eph. 3:17-19

I pray that you grasp what Paul is trying to instill in you, in this scripture. Know that God is always here, ever-present, right where we are. I want to repeat, that no matter what the world says or does or thinks, they cannot stop God. God will always surpass the knowledge of mankind. Though the world explodes with craziness, take your eyes off the craziness and trust that the unstoppable God loves you and wants to be rooted inside of you. You do not need to see or understand or grasp God in your hand. You can trust that His love will not fail. God will not fail you. YES!

6—GOD IS IN MOTION

I have just returned from a trip to Spain and Italy. It was my first time traveling to another continent. My trip was inspired by my daughter who, in her first year of college, was offered the opportunity to go to Italy with a group from school, led by one of her favorite instructors. Although we did not give her permission to go at that time, we did promise her that if she completed her bachelor's degree, we would get her to Italy. And, as you've guessed, she did finish her degree. Not knowing when we would have this opportunity again, we tried to fit three countries into ten days. Don't laugh, a girl can dream. We did settle on two countries in sixteen days.

My favorite tour brought us to the Basilica of the Sagrada Familia in Barcelona, Spain. It is the largest unfinished Catholic Church, designed by the architect Antoni Gaudi. The church is privately owned and financed by donations.

Construction progress is slow as donations trickle in. Construction began in 1882 (131 years ago). Gaudi died in 1926, after only seeing one face of the church completed. They expect to have the full construction complete in 2026, the one hundredth anniversary of Gaudi's death. The first part of our tour took us around the outside of the building, where each side portrays either the birth, life, death, or resurrection of Jesus. The twelve towers represent the twelve apostles while the four central towers represent the evangelists Matthew, Mark, Luke, and John. The tallest tower at the center represents Christ. Every detail of every side is full of purpose and meaning and beauty.

My brief synopsis does not do justice to the fabulous architecture and beauty of this church. I saw pictures on the internet before we went to the cathedral, but they did not prepare me for the moment I walk inside, listening to the guide describing the purpose behind the architects designs for the stained glass windows, columns and ceiling. I cannot even attempt to put into words how I felt as I turned and saw the beautiful light streaming through the glass. Even as I sit here typing, I am overwhelmed with the emotions of my experience. Twenty-first century churches are moving away from using stained glass windows, which were originally introduced in the mid-1100's to teach the Bible to those who could not read. Though I too had seen no need for continuing the tradition, I saw the importance of the stained glass in the Sangrada Familia, which is best described by the artist as "symphonies of colours." So incredibly beautiful and well planned is this cathedral that it creates an ambience of worship that can only be experienced while in the presence of this extremely meaningful structure, truly an anointed gift.

I believe it is worth exploring and looking more closely at the "symphonies of colour". Where do all the beautiful colors come from? I must tell you; it did not come from the idyllic colored glass. Color comes from light, specifically from the motion of light. Without light, the glass would be colorless.

Allow me to share this example of motion. When I was in junior high school, my science teacher took our class to the edge of the blacktop (blacktop is what we called the asphalt area, where the basketball courts and other activities were located). We traveled to where the blacktop met the field of grass. Our teacher handed his assistant a starter pistol and asked him to run to the chain-link fence at the end of the field, to raise the pistol in the air, and to fire it. We all waited for Chancy. That's not his name. I don't remember his name, but Chancy sounds like a good name for an assistant – I digress. While we waited, Mr. D told us that as soon as we saw the smoke from the pistol, he would start the stopwatch, and as soon as we heard the sound of the pistol bang, he would stop the timer. He then asked us to guess how much time had passed between the sight of the smoke and the sound of the shot. He smirked at our inability to judge how much time had passed. As it turned out, all our guesses were way overstated. The elapse had been seconds, not minutes. Nonetheless, he proved that light waves are faster than sound waves. This demonstration was our introduction to wavelengths, which are a characteristic of light.

To further explore these wavelengths, we did another experiment. Back in the classroom, we turned off the lights. Then, using a flashlight to shine through a prism, we could see that what appears from our flashlight as white light, spreads *through* the prism and comes out the other end as a rainbow of colors. The rainbow represents the light separated into its numerous frequencies of energy or wavelengths, called the "spectrum of light". According to some sources (see: https://amazing-space.stsci.edu), one wavelength equals the distance between two successive wave crests or troughs. Frequency (Hertz) equals the number of waves that pass a given point per second. How in the world did someone find and measure all of this? I don't know. What I do know is that without light, there are no colors *and* that light is constantly in motion. Immensely complex yet, measurably consistent.

Life is always in motion with its peaks and with its valleys. We have the wavelengths of seasons; with hot, getting hotter, then too hot – to cooler, getting cold, then too cold. In the summer, I long for cooler days. Winter in California is not as extreme as in other states. Consequently, winter is my favorite season of the year because it is cool enough that I can wear a sweater. I overheat easily and unfortunately; I am not only uncomfortable in the heat but the perspiration gathering on my face is often embarrassing. That matters to me because layers look more stylish. And I want to look well put together. So, I long for those winter months. But winter does not last.

The economy moves in wavelengths. With eight years of recession and then eight years of inflation, we need both. But neither inflation nor recession should last forever. The fluctuations help steer us towards balance. Sadly, we keep passing by balance, so the pendulum must eventually swing back the other way. We have days we are madly in love and days we are terribly angry; days we laugh when wonderful things are happening and days we cry from great loss. And I must say that it is okay to cry. It is not only good for your complexion, but crying is cleansing for the soul. There is a season for everything, as expressed in Ecclesiastes.

> *There is a time for everything, and a season for every activity under the heavens:*
>
> *2 a time to be born and a time to die, a time to plant and a time to uproot,*
>
> *3 a time to kill and a time to heal, a time to tear down and a time to build,*

4 a time to weep and a time to laugh,
a time to mourn and a time to dance,

5 a time to scatter stones and a time to
gather them,
a time to embrace and a time to refrain
from embracing,

6 a time to search and a time to give up,
a time to keep and a time to throw away,

7 a time to tear and a time to mend,
a time to be silent and a time to speak,

8 a time to love and a time to hate,
a time for war and a time for peace.

Eccl. 3:1-8

Understand that it is the motion of wavelengths that brings color. Without the highs and the lows, we have nothing. No motion, no color. If we can hold on to the fact that difficulties will not last, we have grasped hope. While enjoying the highs, remember they also will not last. So, we plan and prepare and brace ourselves for the ride.

We must have change to see the beauty. Life is in motion – it's a good thing. Because that motion is a symphony of color. And, with every change we may get knocked down. We can cry, because there is a time to cry, but remember you should not stay there. We do not need to stay there. We need to pray and then we need to trust that our God of light will carry us through. He will light our path and restore our sight of the amazing colors he has for us. God will make it good. Am I sure about that? Yeah, I am!

Friends, joy is not because of stuff. Joy is because we endure. *And* we can have joy *in* the ride. The book of James says this:

> *Because you know that the testing of your faith produces perseverance.* James 1:3

Do you know that? Do you? Bad stuff is going to happen, and not just to you. Bad stuff happens to everyone. Everyone, great and small must bear something. Everyone. But like the freezing temperature of winter, it will not last. We need to learn to persevere. We can persevere—meaning, we keep moving forward. Keep reading from James.

*Let Perseverance finish its work so that
you may be mature and complete, not
lacking in anything.* James 1:4

Did you hear it? He said "let." That means you
have a choice to make, because even if you choose
to cling to your hurt, the pendulum will continue
to move on, and you will be stagnant and lacking.
Are you willing to move forward? Do you want to
be mature and complete?

When you apply for a job, what is the first
thing they want to know? They want to know
whether you have experience. Experience brings
us to maturity. Experience means you have been
through trial and error and discovery. Our teen-
agers think they have it all figured out and we
smirk. We smirk because until you have dealt with
buying a car, you do not know the proper way to
negotiate. When you graduate from college, you
only know a small fraction of what your profes-
sion will entail. You need experience. Textbook
knowledge is nothing compared to life knowledge. It can take years, maybe even decades for
your knowledge to be complete, and even then,
regulations or technology or something else can

change, because life is in motion and change is inevitable. So, you learn more.

Let's continue to the next verse in the passage.

> *If any of you lacks wisdom, you should*
> *ask God, who gives generously to all*
> *without finding fault, and it will be*
> *given you.* James 1:5

Thank you, God. How many times have I prayed this prayer? "God help me. I know I'm the idiot that got me in this mess, and I know you've helped me a multitude of times before. I don't deserve your help, but please help me, help me, help me!" You guessed it–God helps a knucklehead. Though it is my fault, he helps without finding fault. Thank you, God for giving me the wisdom I need!

> *But when you ask, you must believe*
> *and not doubt, because the one who*
> *doubts is like a wave of the sea, blown*
> *and tossed by the wind. That person*
> *should not expect to receive anything*

from the Lord. Such a person is dou-
ble-minded and unstable in all they do.
James 1:6-8

The waves of the sea are not consistent like light waves. The sea can gently rock you or toss you from side to side or a storm can damage your boat. You can trust God because he is light, and we know light is consistent. God is better than an anchor preventing you from drifting. When you trust God, you will not only survive, you will be better because of it. I know many of you can name tragedies that, as far as you can see, cannot possibly have a good outcome. But I guarantee that whatever tragedy you are amid, someone else has not only been there, but is an overcomer. Look for them. Be inspired. Find your purpose. Be an overcomer and share your story of how God took you through. You may have been humbled, take pride in your humble circumstances.

Take pride in your humble circum-
stance and the rich should take pride in
their humiliation because like the wild-
flower, in the scorching heat the plant

*will wither; its blossoms will fall, and its
beauty destroyed.* James 1:9-11

Things do not last. Empires can be built and
can be destroyed. As I told my children repeatedly,
everything is breakable. We want to take pride
in our great achievements, but remember pride
comes before the fall. Wavelengths. Do not mis-
take humiliation as being the same as a doormat
or as giving up or giving in. It's not. Humiliation
is wisdom, the realization that things can change,
for you and for others. But despite your situation,
you can be content and can continue into the next
wave, keep moving forward. Take pride in your
humble circumstance, it comes with a blessing.

*Blessed is the one who perseveres under
trial because, having stood the test, that
person will receive the crown of life that
the Lord has promised to those who love
him.* James 1:12

As I said earlier, real joy comes when we
endure. When a man climbs Kilimanjaro, he
smiles and laughs and jumps for joy, not as much
for the amazing view as for the fact that he made

it to the top. A climber prepares ahead of time for the climb. They will spend months hiking, then hiking with a backpack. They will then hike in higher altitudes and increase their endurance. Kilimanjaro is at an extreme altitude and even a well-trained climber can get what is called "acute mountain sickness." But when you make it to the top, you can shout, Halleluiah! Your Kilimanjaro may not be an actual mountain, but it can sure feel like one. Whether you're in an accident or lose a loved one, you can make it. Ask God. He will help you in ways you cannot imagine. And here is the best part:

> *Every good and perfect gift is from above, coming down from the Father of the heavenly lights, who does not change like shifting shadows.* James 1:17

Did that click? Read it again. The Father of the heavenly lights, who does NOT change! Throughout the Bible, God tells us He does not change. You do not need to stare at the sun to know that there is light. You can see the colors of life around you and you *know* there is light. You cannot grasp it in your hand, but it's there. And

51

because of the light of God, because you trust His light, you will grow and become a better version of you. You will be stronger and taller, and you will be radiant with joy. Embrace the light. Keep moving forward. Walk in the light and let your light shine. In the light of God, you can enjoy symphonies of color!

7—GOD IS PURE ENERGY

G rowing up I would sit at the dining room table and do my homework. When I got to a fact I did not know or a word I could not spell, I would ask my mom for help and she would say, "Look it up." So, I would get my lazy bottom out of the chair and walk those three long steps to the dictionary. My father, who loved to build things, made a podium that had just the right sized top, to hold our extremely large, unabridged dictionary. When closed, it was of considerable proportions, about 10" wide by 14" or 15" tall and about 6" thick. It was big and heavy and sat on its own prominent display in our dining room. I had a desk in my room, but it saved time and energy to sit at the dining room table near the dictionary. I tell my children, it is my mom's fault, that in every argument we have about facts, I google it. That's right, I look it up – or do the modern equivalent. Drives them crazy. "Mom, we need to take Google away from you!" Yes, fun fact. Well, fun fact to me. I'm smiling right now as I write this. I want to giggle because – well I just did.

My brother shared with me an article he read years ago about a group of scientists that built some giant magnets to see if they could create matter. And, because it matters to my next point—yes, pun intended—you know what I did? That's right, I googled it. I found that in March of 2010, NDTV wrote an article entitled, "Big Bang Experiment Successful."

The European Organization for Nuclear Research (CERN) built the world's largest and most powerful particle accelerator, named "Large Hadron Collider," near Geneva, 300 feet below ground, in a 17-mile long ring of superconducting magnets. Whoa, seventeen miles of magnets. I don't think I can even see seventeen miles away.

In the experiment, they used the magnets to force two beams of proton particles to collide. The beams were moving nearly at the speed of light, though in opposite directions. In case it's been awhile since high school science class, every solid, liquid, gas, and plasma are composed of atoms. Atoms are made of protons, electrons, and neutrons. Protons and electrons are made up of quarks—not quirks, quarks— (though I find quarks quirky). Not funny? Okay, back to Geneva. The main purpose was for scientist to see what might have happened in the first split seconds of the creation of the universe, according to the "big bang" theory. The article states that they had additional goals beyond finding the Higgs Boson, or the so-called "God particle," the "God particle" being the origin of mass. They wanted to examine the nature of matter and the origins of stars and planets, and possibly new discoveries in the laws of physics. The experiment was successful in that the proton beams did cross and microscopic particles did collide. They continue to experiment with greater numbers of proton particles, like billions at a time.

Did I mention that it took twenty-five years and ten billion dollars to build this particle accelerator? My brother brilliantly pointed something out. For these scientists to attempt to create mass, they needed seventeen miles of superconductive magnets, which accelerated moving particles up to 99.999999% of the speed of light. Wrap your brain around that one. What they proved is that you cannot make something out of nothing. You cannot have a big bang, until you have something to create the big bang, and not a little something, but an enormous, seventeen-mile-long, something. That's 5,280 feet times 17 equals 89,760 feet of super-conducting magnets to create a mass so small, that you need a microscope to see it. It blows me away to think about it. If it took that much energy to create a microscopic speck of mass, how much energy would it take to create a flower? Even more astounding is the question, how much energy would it take to create a star? Talk about intelligent, *intentional* design! I for one, am not afraid to call that intelligence "God."

God is light, and light is pure energy. God is pure energy. Pure ENERGY. Some light is visible, such as the colors you can see with the naked eye. Tighter, faster wavelengths cannot be seen by our eyes. This light is used for x-rays. Slower, broader lengths, that are also invisible, are used for microwaves and radios. Some light is visible while some light is invisible. I will say it again: light is pure energy. The invisible God of light is pure energy.

Moses wanted to see God. He literally heard God's voice on a regular basis, but he wanted more. How very human of him! Most of us have broken down and said it too. "Lord, are you really there? I can't see you." Or: "Lord give me a sign."

So, Moses in Exodus 33 is talking with God, and God tells him 'My presence will go with you, and I will give you rest.' And Moses is saying (I paraphrase), "yeah, yeah, you're pleased with me, you're with me, I want more." Then he says, "Now show me your glory."

> *And the Lord said, "I will cause all my goodness to pass in front of you, and I will proclaim my name, the Lord, in your presence. I will have mercy on whom I will have mercy, and I will have compassion on whom I will have compassion. But," he said, "you cannot see my face, for no one may see me and live."* Ex. 33:19-20

God's energy is so intense that we cannot handle it. But God understood Moses desire and gave him this option. God tells Moses to go to this rock with a cleft in it, and when He passes by the rock, He will cover Moses with His hand until He has passed by. Then He would remove His hand and Moses would see God's back or, His passing glory. And Moses goes for it. What Moses did not realize until he came back down the mountain, was that his face was now glowing—not like your sweaty face in the sunlight, but rather his face was radiant. All the Israelites, including his brother Aaron, were afraid to come near him, so Moses wore a veil to make it more comfortable for people to come close. This story explains why angels glow and how the sun, moon, and stars got their shine. They were created by the most powerful source of energy, the glorious light of God. The Book of Revelation tells us:

> *The city does not need the sun or the moon to shine on it, for the glory of God gives it light, and the Lamb is its lamp.*
> Rev. 21:23

God is greater than seventeen miles of magnets. He is greater than anything we can think or imagine. His energy gave light to the sun and all stars. This energy is His glory. And he used the vessel, Jesus the Lamb not only to hold light and to spread light but to gives us a greater connection to God. God's Holy Spirit is that bit of God's light inside of us. Our source of strength. Our rescue and refuge from the darkness of this world.

The Lord is my light and my salvation – whom shall I fear? The Lord is the stronghold of my life – of whom shall I be afraid? Ps 27:1

I am quite sure the psalmist David, the shepherd boy, did not study physics. Yet he knew where his strength and salvation came from. He trusted in the power of God's light. Whom shall I fear? Because greater is He that is in me, than he that is in the world. Seventeen miles of magnets created a mere micro-speck of mass. God created the sun, moon, and stars. His power and his energy far exceed our comprehension. We have nothing to fear because God is greater. Whatever it is you are going through, trust that our God is not only with you, but that God is making a way for you to come out the other side, stronger and wiser. I love the song by Kelly Willard that says:

I will cast all my cares upon you. I'll lay all of my burdens down at your feet. And anytime I don't know what to do. I will cast all my cares upon you.

Know that God is your light and your salvation. Embrace what we have learned so far. God is the light that gives us sight and balance. He is the light that is constant and where we will learn everything. God's light is in motion, putting color and joy in our lives. God is pure energy. Though He is invisible, He is absolutely, unequivocally, right where you are. And the power of God, in the form of the Holy Spirit, can dwell in us. Nothing is more powerful. Nothing can stop the love of God which is shown to us in Christ Jesus. Hallelujah!

8—GOD IS EVERYWHERE

I magine you are walking through a thick forest at night. Nothing scary in the forest, only darkness—unless you are flat out afraid of the dark. But I promise, right here, right now, there is no boogeyman in this forest. Walk with me. We'll go together. Did I mention I get lost easily? Now you are wishing you had taken this hike with someone else, but you are stuck with me. Good news, up ahead we can see light. Yes, we will walk towards the light. Which happens to be the point of this book: we need to walk towards the light. But not the point of this chapter. Guess what? Yes, I googled again, "How far away can we see light?" Here is what I found. A six-foot-tall person can see the horizon from a little over three miles away. However, our visual acuity extends far beyond the horizon. For instance, if you are on top of a mountain, the horizon can be hundreds of miles away. One source believes we could see a candle flame flickering up to thirty miles away, provided it is dark everywhere else. Now that we know we can find light, we just need to look for light and head towards it.

Let's get back to the forest. When we get to the clearing, where we can see the building from which the light is coming, we can also see that the door to this building is open. Through the opening, it appears as if the light bends around the edges of the doorway, or glows beyond. This effect is called "diffraction". Because light is a wave, it can "bend" around a corner. On the ground you can see that as the light gets further away from the door, it becomes less intense. If you turn around and look at the forest behind you, you can see the trees and may even make out the individual leaves from that glow. The incredible thing is that though the source of light is not directed to shine out the door; though the lamp in the room is not intended to light anything other than the room where it is located; from the radiance of that lamp, we see the path.

Multiply the intensity of the lamp by I don't know how much, and you have the radiance of the sun. I read that if we made a ball of 100-watt, incandescent light bulbs, it would have to be somewhere around 45,000 times *bigger* than the sun, to be *as* bright as the sun. YIKES! That's intense. Literally. This required magnitude for the light bulbs also shows us that our own manufactured power, in the 100W bulb, is nothing in comparison to the power of the sun, created by the power of God. And, God's power is immeasurably greater than the suns'!

> *The Son is the radiance of God's glory and the exact representation of his being, sustaining all things by his powerful word. After he had provided purification for sins, he sat down at the right hand of the Majesty in heaven.* Heb. 1:3

When Hebrews says, *"The Son is the* radiance *of God's glory,"* he is telling us, the source of light (God) and the radiance (the Son) are one, just as stated in the Gospel of John: "In the beginning was the Word, and the Word was with God, and the Word was God." You can't have light without radiance nor radiance without light. Hebrews goes on to say:

and the exact representation of his being, sustaining all things by his powerful word. Heb. 1:3

My favorite quote ever, came from a *Reader's Digest* back in the 70's, from an unknown author. I memorized it and took it to heart.

Jesus is God spelling himself out in a language man can understand.

Or in the words of John,

The true light, *which gives light to everyone, was coming into the world.* John 1:9

This verse speaks of Jesus. God puts on human form, living what we live, feeling what we feel, and then showing us how to live. Wow! Human beings do not understand the invisible God, so God puts on skin and shows us exactly who he is and how immensely he loves us, by radiating through Jesus.

Jesus loved the tax collector and took the time to eat with him, talk with him and show him a better life. He felt the touch of the woman who needed healing. She was healed. He reached out to those who, by human standards, were unlovable. Jesus showed them love—not by joining in their depravity, but by showing them the way out. Christ not only showed great love when He sacrificed himself as our sin offering – he went more than a step beyond, when on the cross, he forgave. To the thief He said,

> *Today you will be with me in paradise.*
> Luke 23:43

Today. Jesus knew the thief's heart and He said, today. To what seemed like the end, Jesus continued to show intense love and unfathomable forgiveness. But it was not the end! Jesus, the radiance of God, still shines and the extension of that light, in the form of the Holy Spirit, lives in me. YES! Fist pump! I have the power of God in me.

I pray you too have chosen to absorb the light and allow the radiance to grow and to glow. The sustainer of light, the sustainer of life, will sustain you. There is nothing you will face alone. And God will give you the power to successfully overcome whatever problem you may be up against or dispel any weakness you may have.

God is not constrained to a vessel, like a bulb of light. His energy is everywhere. He formed the universe, brought life to the earth. Not only did God create, he also sustains life. He used a smidge of his energy to impregnate Mary, so he could show us who he is through the human form of Jesus. And, God can seep into your skin and penetrate your heart, filling it with his Holy Spirit. One light reaching us in three ways, that creates life and color and joy. You are never alone. *God is everywhere*, all at the same time. Stretching beyond what we can see, think, or imagine.

9–GOD GIVES US PERSPECTIVE

My children went to a Christian elementary school and every year, from kindergarten through sixth grade, they participated in a speech meet. The child with the top score would go on to compete in a District Speech Meet. When my son was in the sixth grade, his teacher gave him the tale by Aesop "The Ant and The Grasshopper" for the meet, only retold by Rohini Chowdhury. It wasn't until today that I found out that Aesop's version is much shorter than this retelling by Rohini. That would only matter to my son and me because, the contestants had to keep their speech within five-minutes. Once my son memorized and then animated his speech with facial expressions and hand gestures, we worked hard to get this speech to a length under five-minutes. We even asked the teacher if he could have a shorter speech, but she said no–that he should embrace the challenge.

On the day of the competition my son was on fire. He quoted the speech as fast as he could, while still bringing life to the story. I was so proud. Afterwards we read each judges' comments. All stated that he was amazing, the best they had ever heard, and he should have won but, his speech ran four seconds over the five allotted minutes. Ugh!

Aesop's telling is 282 words while Rohini's is 452. Aesop got right to the point. "There is a time for work and a time for play," and the ants walked away from the grasshopper, and that was that. Rohini expanded upon how much the grasshopper played day after day, and how the ants worked day after day, each finding the other lacking, and therefore mocking their choices. From the ant's perspective, it is most important to plan and work towards that plan. Like the Boy Scouts, the ant wanted to be prepared. From the grasshopper's perspective, the future is not today, so today I will play. When winter came the grasshopper had no food nor shelter and Rohini gets into the emotions of the choices each made before coming to the same conclusion intended by Aesop. There is a time for work and a time for play. It is all about perspective. Two extreme, opposite perspectives on what is important to do today. We are inundated with opposing perspectives. I implore that you will conclude that the only perspective that matters is Gods.

We can have different perspectives on what we physically see. As a kid, I remember staring at the fish tank in the doctor's waiting room. Looking at a fish, depending on where I stood, I could tell that the fish was not seen in its actual location. And in school, I remember my teacher putting a pencil partially in a glass of water. At the top of the water, as one looked at the side of the glass, it appeared that the water was splitting the pencil. The top half, above the water, did not line up with the lower half, below the water. Refraction is a phenomenon whereby light reacts with water and changes the way we see things. Light interacts with matter, whether by bending a pencil or bursting through the clouds in radiant beams of light or as the colors in a rainbow. From the side of the fish tank you experience refraction. But get on a step stool to look down over the top of the tank and you clearly see where the fish is. Where you stand affects your perspective. God is looking down from above. He sees exactly where we are because He has the best view. The light of God, which gives us balance, life, energy, and sight, also gives us true, clear, perspective.

God interacts with us regardless of our response and whether we choose to interact with him or not—because God, just as light, is physically and mentally in every aspect of life. As Paul reminds us in Romans:

> *Since what may be known about God is plain to them, because God has made it plain to them. For since the creation of the world God's invisible qualities-his eternal power and divine nature-have been clearly seen, being understood from what has been made, so that men are without excuse.* Rom. 1: 19-20

God has already revealed himself to you. He is pursuing you. His plan for you is perfect because He has the best perspective. His energy formed the sun, moon, and stars. God's light breathed life into everything. I encourage you to pursue him with all your heart, soul, mind, and strength.

For with you is the fountain of life; in your light, we see light. Ps 36:9

Our perspective can be altered by where we choose to plant ourselves. In God's light we see truth. Darkness is in the evil one. Division is Satan's greatest tool. United in Christ we should stand because divided in darkness we will fall. From the separation of Adam and Eve from the truth of God; then the first recorded injustice between Cain and Abel, Satan works to divide us, to skew our perspective. Truth is in God's light. I may not be making myself clear, but God can make everything clear. God wants us to stand in His light, not so that he can control us, because he does not. He lets us choose. When you tell a three-year-old not to touch the hot stove, is it to control or to help them? Your perspective of the hot stove is different than the curious three-year-old's. And even if you tell him not to, he may still touch the stove, because he can choose to do so.

God is great and has used the prophets to write wisdom, in the form of the scriptures of the Bible. We must pray and read Gods word. God is faithful, unchanging, ever-present, all-power, all around us. GOD IS LIGHT! There will come a day when we will see God, face to face, and everything will make complete sense and we will enjoy absolute balance and perspective. Until then, our choices and life itself will swing in directions that will be difficult for us. But God will show us the way to be overcomers. His power will sustain us. We will be more than conquerors–not just conquerors but more than conquerors, much more! A conqueror wins a battle, but that is not the end of all battles. We know who wins in the end. God, from the vantage point of everywhere, because He is everywhere, giving us clarity and purpose and life.

10–GOD IS LIGHT.

I am a 5'-1 1/2" Hispanic female. I was born in Los Angeles County and went to school in Orange County. Because my older brother, who was born in Puerto Rico, was beat-up for not knowing English, my father declared that there would be no more Spanish spoken in our house. My older brother and sister lost the ability to speak the Spanish language, while my younger brother and I never learned Spanish at all. I know my older brother and sister had more struggles than I did. We grew up in a predominantly Anglo neighborhood and schools. And the experience of being an ethnic minority affected me enough that, at first, I started to write this book under the name "Annie", instead of Juanita, my actual name. I felt that because my name is Hispanic, I would not be taken seriously. After all, my past has left a scar.

How many times did God use the most unlikely people to be his prophets, leaders, disciples, or heroes? In this time of my life, when I am much older and a little wiser, I believe everyone has a story, some worse than others but all of us have faced trials. And it is because of my experiences, that I can relate to Moses' fear of being used by God to lead His people. I am not saying I have been called to lead, I'm only saying I understand Moses' fear of being asked to lead.

In Exodus 3 we read about Moses while he was tending his father-in-law's sheep. Moses leads the flock to the far side of the desert, all the way to Horeb, known as the mountain of God. It is here that he sees a flame of fire inside of a bush but the bush itself was not being consumed by the fire. Intrigued, he decides to take a closer look. God sees that He has Moses' attention and then speaks to him. In this holy moment God not only lets Moses know that he hears the cries of His enslaved, oppressed people, but also that He wants Moses to lead His people out of Egypt to a land of milk and honey. Moses does not believe that he is up to this task of leadership and throughout the chapter, he questions God's election of him as a leader. And in response to Moses' concern that the Israelites will want evidence that it is their God who sends him, Moses asks, "What shall I tell them is your name?" Of the many names of God – Wonderful, Counselor, Almighty, Everlasting Father, Prince of Peace, Master, Most High, Provider, Healer, Sanctifier, Lord of Hosts, Shepherd, Righteous – the name which God supplies to Moses, is the one name that sums up all names. This name is God's ultimate name.

> God said to Moses, "I AM WHO I AM. This is what you are to say to the Israelites: 'I AM has sent me to you.'" Ex. 3:14

I AM. God is the *great* <u>I AM.</u> What more can I say? God created the heavens and the earth because He is the ultimate source of energy and life–He is THE Light. Not a singular light, like a flashlight or the sun, but THE Light, the energy that has always been and always will be and is everything and everywhere, the Great I AM!

> Send me your light and your faithful care, let them lead me; let them bring me to your holy mountain, to the place where you dwell. Ps. 43:3

Send me your light, give me more of you God; *and your faithful care*, God's constant, faithful, ever-present care that we may have abundant life. *Let them lead me*, God will faithfully show us the way to the top of the holy mountain where we can rejoice because we are overcomers. God's faithful care is the light that shines, the light that directs, the light that fills our lives with joy! And God wants to shine his light through us.

> *I, the Lord, have called you in righteousness; I will take hold of your hand. I will keep you and will make you to be a covenant for the people and a light for the Gentiles.* Isa. 42:6

To be a light for others is not exclusive to the Old Testament. The apostle Matthew also wrote:

> *In the same way, let your light shine before others, that they may see your good deeds and glorify your Father in heaven.* Matt 5:16

Let your light shine – let the goodness of God shine through you. You've seen them, I've seen them; those people that you look at, who have this glow on their face, and we think, "that person looks like a Christian". God's light can shine through us. We may not have the exuberant face, but the light can shine through us when we help those in need, even in simple acts of kindness. It is super easy to gossip and tear down everyone and anyone, but super Christ-like to build people up. Show mercy, promote gentleness. Give them a kind word, share what you have, a smile. Here is one of my favorite lines from Buddy the Elf:

I just like to smile, smiling's my favorite.

There is a lot of light that radiates from a smile. I once had a professor who challenged us to smile at a stranger as we walked past them. As he predicted, they would smile back. Don't be stingy with your smiles.

My father was the last person I would have expected to be a tool of inspiration. But, as I sat between my two brothers one July afternoon, God used my father, a most unlikely person, to speak to me. You never know when you may be influencing others. That gives even more reason to let your light shine before men, that they may see your good works and glorify your Father who is everywhere!

This powerful scripture from the prologue of the gospel of John, explores The Light even further.

In the beginning was the Word, John 1:1a

Word with a capital W – the Word is Jesus, who is "God spelling himself out in a language man can understand."

> *and the Word was with God, and the Word was God. He was with God in the beginning.* John 1:1b-2

How can the Word be both "along-side God" and God himself, as the verse tells us? Go outside on a sunny day and turn on a flashlight. Now tell me, which light is from the sun and which is from the flashlight? Light blends with light. It is like pouring water into water. Once both portions of water are in the glass you cannot tell the two apart. God the father and God the son is one light; they are one God.

Through him all things were made; without him nothing was made that has been made. In him was life, and that life was the light of men. John 1:3-4

That's right–life. Remember Chapter Four, light is life, God is light, God is life. *And that life was the light of men.* Pause and soak this in. The light of men. THE light. Again, not a flashlight or a light bulb or any other imitation of light that humans can create from materials that God has given to us. He is *the light*. He is greater, *far* greater, than the sunlight because he is the power, and the energy, that has created that light and all light. And He wants to illuminate you.

The light shines in the darkness, but the darkness has not understood it. John 1:5

A group from the Massachusetts Institute of Technology did an experiment, posting two articles on social media. One was true and the other was not. The article that was a lie was visited and reposted ten times more than the truth. *But the darkness does not understand.* Sometimes it is because people don't want to understand. And sometimes things are incomprehensible. Can we really comprehend the sun? Scientists think that the sun is the biggest source of energy in the universe. The huge glowing sphere of hot gas, which just happens to be there? No. You think the sun is big? Our God is greater. The sun is a tiny speck compared to God, the very source of all light. YES! If seventeen miles of magnets creates a speck of mass, how incredibly big is the God who created the sun? Indescribably large. We cannot fully comprehend God.

> *There came a man who was sent from God; his name was John. He came as a witness to testify concerning that light, so that through him all men might believe.* John 1:6-7

The world, governed by the prince of darkness, has tried to cover up the light. They won't let our faith be shared in schools and then blame our morality problems on objects, not on the hearts that reject the Light. Drugs are illegal, yet we still have a horrible drug problem, because bottom line, we have a morality problem. But we who love the Light must be a witness for that Light. Let your light shine.

> *He himself was not the light; he came only as a witness to the light. The true light that gives light to every man was coming into the world.* John 1:8-9

John the Baptist is not himself the light. Of course not, John was created by the light as we were. John not only accepted the light into himself, he knew his purpose was to be a witness of the light. John knew Jesus is the light and he did not hold it in.

> *He was in the world, and though the world was made through him, the world did not recognize him.* John 1:10

I pray that you recognize God. That you seek His balance and life; that you sense His ever-present energy and motion. And though you cannot grasp God in your hand or see His invisible energy, you will have confidence in His consistency. Recognize His faithful care and appreciate that in God, is where the best perspective exists, for our good. The world's light is like a Bic lighter. Don't be fooled by the world's little Bic lighter. Because that is all the power this world has. It is nothing compared to the Light of God, the source of color and of life and the true power and knowledge beyond our finite minds.

> *He came to that which was his own, but his own did not receive him. Yet to all who received him, to those who believe in his name, he gave the right to become children of God – children born not of natural descent, nor of human decision or a husband's will, but born of God.* John 1:11-13

Can I hear an "Amen" or "Right On!" or a "thank you, Jesus!"? We don't have to fumble through life. We get to be children of the almighty – <u>ALL</u> Mighty!

> *The Word became flesh and made his dwelling among us. We have seen his glory, the glory of the One and Only, who came from the Father, full of grace and truth.* John 1:14

I need to repeat that–We have seen his glory, HIS glory, His magnificence, His beauty, the glory of the One and Only, who came from the Father, full of grace and truth. Even people we might call "good people" need grace. How many times have I driven over the speed limit or gossiped–you know, sharing information that is true about someone but that brings them down – things people say that are hurtful and sometimes harmful. I am not as kind to my husband as I should be. Arguments come from selfishness, the desire to have our own way. I wish I had given my children more time, more hugs, I wish I could have made them feel more important. There are a million things we expect to have grace for. We all have something we would never want to come back on us. Yet, we expect to be called "good". We need grace. On the flip side, when you receive grace, accept it. Guilt erases grace. Accept grace and walk away from guilt because Truth with a capital T has grace for you. Thank God He has grace for me.

> *John testifies concerning him. He cries*
> *out saying, "This was he of whom I said,*
> *'He who comes after me has surpassed*
> *me because he was before me'. From the*

fullness of his grace we all receive one blessing after another. For the law was given through Moses; grace and truth came through Jesus Christ. No one has ever seen God, but God the One and Only, who is at the Fathers side, has made him known. John 1:15-18

From the fullness of His grace we all receive one blessing after another. I have seen God's hand in my life. Like you, I have a story. But rather than focus on the tragedies of my life, I choose Light. I choose to count my blessings, one after another. I cannot see God physically, but I can see the colors of life. Is my life perfect? Of course not. Am I perfect? Of course not. But I have God's grace and truth moving me through it all.

The sun will no more be your light by day, nor will the brightness of the moon shine on you, for the Lord will be your everlasting light, and your God will be your glory. Your sun will never set again, and your moon will wane no more; the Lord will be your everlasting

light, and your days of sorrow will end.
Isa 60:19-20

Open your eyes, your heart, and your mind, to the hope of glory. This generation will pass. But, praise God, we who believe, who are children of God, will blend into the light of glory. The Light of God with no beginning and no end. Amen? Yes, Amen!

In summary, this is what I hope you take away from what I have shared. I am sure that you who are physicists can come up with a longer list, but let's review what we've learned from my limited knowledge of light.

LIGHT not only helps us to see where we are going, but it keeps us from walking in circles.

1. GOD IS BALANCE. We need light to see and direct us from walking in circles. Balance is important. Despite our choices, the choices of others or the circumstances of life, God can restore our balance. His Word directs and protects and unites us with others, He can provide balance with family, friends, faith, and forgiveness, and

in the balance of contentment, we will have the best life.

LIGHT is the only constant in the universe, so everything is measured or calibrated against the speed of light. Most of what scientists know about the universe comes from information that has been carried to us by light.

2. GOD IS CONSTANT. God is the same yesterday, today and forever. Life is full of change, but God never changes. As our creator, everything is measured and calibrated through him because *all* knowledge is in him. We can have confidence in God's constant nature, how great is His faithfulness.

We need LIGHT to grow.

3. GOD IS LIFE. In the beginning God created the heavens and the earth. Darkness was over the surface of the earth and God said, "Let there be light". Light had to be next because without light, there is no life. What I hope I have clearly expressed is this:

Light is life, God is light, <u>God is life</u>. And a healthy life is not only watered by His word, but lets it soak deep inside, that you may overflow with joy!

LIGHT has no mass.

4. GOD IS WITHOUT MASS. God cannot be grasped, neither physically nor mentally. Though we cannot see Him or touch Him, He is right here, right now and we are in His grasp. No matter what the world says, or does or thinks or demands, they cannot stop God's light from shining. Nothing can stop God.

LIGHT is in motion, through wavelengths of color and unseen energy.

5. GOD IS IN MOTION, moving throughout the universe in colors that are both seen and unseen. One God as one light, spread in the frequencies of Father, Son and Spirit. Each acting through the hills and valleys of our lives, creating symphonies of color. I know that God will make things work

for the good of those who love Him. Keep moving forward.

LIGHT is pure energy.

6. GOD IS PURE ENERGY. God's immense, unfathomable, energy gave power to the sun, moon, and stars. His light is a rainbow of color, both seen and unseen. There is no greater energy than God–*oh my God!* Nothing is more powerful than God.

LIGHT expands beyond its source, even around corners.

7. GOD IS EVERYWHERE. God expands beyond the universe. His light is everywhere, moving everywhere, all at once. Like the earth, it is us who turn away from the Son. God is still there, waiting for us to turn towards His light. He is everywhere and around every corner. You are never alone. God is available and present right where you are, where I am, for each one of us, ready to engulf us with His glorious radiance.

LIGHT interacts with matter.

8. GOD GIVES US PERSPECTIVE. God sees the big picture – He sees the entire picture. To help our perspective, God essentially put on skin, in the form of Jesus, and dwelt among us. He interacted not only with his apostles and disciples but with anyone asking for His attention. When Jesus left His skin, by dying on the cross as our sin offering, God's light came to us in the form of the Holy Spirit. The Holy Spirit reacts and interacts with our hearts and enlightens the way we see things, by giving us a perspective of the big picture as we search God's word. He gives us clarity and purpose and life.

This knowledge has expanded my understanding of the word omnipotent – unlimited power. When you compare the power of seventeen miles of magnets to create a microscopic spec or creating a ball made of 100-watt light bulbs, in order to be as bright as the sun, how much more power would it take to create the sun. What does that say about the amount of power to create the universe? Unfathomable. The name of this omnipotence, this pure infinite energy, is God, the power of all power.

God is omniscient – all-knowing. He gives us guidance we as children sometimes rebel against. We rebel and then blame everyone and everything for our imbalance. We need to respond to the truth that God is balance and life. Everything we know is because of God because God is all-knowing.

The best part is His omnipresence—God is constantly encountered. Though God has no mass and cannot be grasped, though His spectrum of motion and energy is invisible to us, He is relentlessly present in my life and in your life and everywhere. God breathed into us, igniting the spark of life. We are more than conquerors through the sacrifice of Jesus, the radiance of God in human form. And He offers us more power when we choose to be filled with the Holy Spirit. Yes!

This is God: The great **I AM**.

CPSIA information can be obtained
at www.ICGtesting.com
Printed in the USA
LVHW080533141120
671499LV00007B/439